Have Hope

A Devotional for Daughters in Christ

Have Hope
Published by Rachael Masters
With Castle Publishing Ltd

New Zealand

© 2022 Rachael Masters

ISBN 978-0-473-62835-2 (Softcover)

Editing: Sally Webster

Design & Layout: Emma Stevens and Dani Codnig

All Scripture quotations, unless otherwise indicated,
are taken from the Holy Bible, New International Version®, NIV®.
Copyright ©1973, 1978, 1984, 2011 by Biblica, Inc.™
Used by permission of Zondervan.

ALL RIGHTS RESERVED

No part of this publication may be reproduced,
stored in a retrieval system, or transmitted
in any form or by any means, electronic, mechanical,
photocopying, recording or otherwise,
without prior written permission from the author.

Contents

Acknowledgements	5
Introduction	7
The Good Secret	8
Forgiving and Forgetting	10
Seek and Find	12
Spread Your Wings	14
Testifying	16
Never Too Young	18
Repentance	20
Jesus Wept	22
In His Image	24
God's Goodness	26
Glory	28
Before The Ring	30
Above All Else	32
Shine!	34
A Higher Plan	36
The Waiting Room	38
Wrong Direction	40
Joy	42
After The Battle	44
Mountain-Climbing	46
Just Ask Jesus	48
Representing God's Love	50
Save Our Souls	52
Whoops!	54
Begin Again	56
The Ways of The World	58
Gracious	60
For Such a Time	62
Called	64
Real Love	66
Be Bold!	68
Princess and the Frog	70
Royal Crown	72
Relational Faith	74
Chickens	76
Open Doors	78
Pointless Worry	80
Modest is Hottest	82
Stand Up	84
Lies	86
Contentment	88
Children of God	90
Acceptance	92
Powerful Words	94
Rest	96
Blessed is She	98
Overcoming Fear	100
Consistency	102
Gratitude	104
Give Your Heart	106

Acknowledgements

My constant helping-hand, Jesus – for guiding me every step of the way.

My wonderful mum, Colleen – for constantly reminding me of the calling God has for me.

My beautiful friends, Emma and Dani – for patiently and creatively illustrating the manuscript.

My talented father, Derek – for drawing the illustrations.

My highschool mentor and spiritual leader, Hannah – who supported me through all of my teenage challenges.

Introduction

Kia ora, my name is Rachael Masters!

I have felt called to write a devotional book ever since I was in high school. Back then, like every other teenager, I experienced the wonders and perplexities of the world in a new way. I turned to devotional books to seek advice on issues such as confidence, identity and how to live out God's calling on my life. As a consequence of what I experienced and learned at that time, I was inspired to write my very own devotional book for girls who, like me, were seeking encouragement in what life was bringing their way.

Have Hope has been created to spark hope in your heart, and to encourage you to pursue the calling God has for you. It is my personal testimony, and has Bible references that I hope will help bring it to life. I believe God can cause all things to work together for good in those who love him (Romans 8:28). May you be blessed as you read these short devotionals with an open heart and allow God to speak to you through them.

The Good Secret

I have a secret to tell you. It's one that my mum once told me, and of which God has reminded me repeatedly: I should speak only words of purity and kindness. My tongue should be used for goodness; no evil should be spoken.

It's easy to gossip and to pass judgement on others. This is especially common with teenagers at school, and even at church. Gossip can so easily creep in. Learning to speak good things to and about others, rather than speaking evil, is one of the best ways to promote life and happiness. Also, it will save you from many uncomfortable situations, and from saying things you might later regret. God has created you to be a light to the world and a friend to others, just like Jesus was. He wants to be able to speak words of life and healing through you. So speak with kindness, just as Jesus did!

The soothing tongue is a tree of life, but a perverse tongue crushes the spirit.
(Proverbs 15:4)

Forgiving and Forgetting

When you don't know how to face it, the past can become one of the biggest bullies in your life, beating you up daily. You may be too scared to think about what happened or what you did in your past, and this may even keep you awake at night.

God wants you to know that you are his child, and that your past can be redeemed and put right. You were created to be the person you are. You may need to forgive someone who has hurt or damaged you, and you may even need to forgive yourself. No matter the shame you may feel, God can use whatever the devil has brought against you and turn it into something that will work for your good. Forgiving is the first step in letting go of the past. Forgetting may well follow. If it's painful to look back on the past, then ask God to heal you. He has promised to set the captives free (see Luke 4:18). He wants you to be at peace with who he made you to be, so call on him. He will teach you how to forgive yourself and others, and how to live in his love.

If we confess our sins, he is faithful and just and will forgive us our sins and purify us from all unrighteousness. (1 John 1:9)

But if you do not forgive others their sins, your Father will not forgive your sins. (Matthew 6:15)

Seek and Find

Ask and it will be given to you; seek and you will find; knock and the door will be opened to you. For everyone who asks receives; the one who seeks finds; and to the one who knocks, the door will be opened. (Matthew 7:7-8 NIV)

These have to be two of my all-time favourite Bible verses. They are special because they tell us that if we seek God, then we will find him. If we seek a relationship with him, we will be given it; if we seek his love, presence and peace, we will experience it. I know it's not always as simple as it seems – we can't always expect to ask for something and the next minute get it. Seeking involves spending time and making an effort. It requires that we spend more time with God. It often calls for the surrendering of those things that aren't part of his plan for us.

If you really desire to build a relationship with the Lord, then I encourage you to truly seek him. He wants a relationship with you.

A tip for you: Go to bed around 15 minutes earlier than usual. Use this time to play worship music, read your Bible and pray. Then journal what God has said to you.

Ask and it will be given to you; seek and you will find; knock and the door will be opened to you. (Matthew 7:7)

Spread Your Wings

After finishing high school I had to make the difficult choice between staying at home with my parents or moving out and relocating to a completely new city. At the time I felt that God was telling me that I needed to spread my wings and fly. It frightened me to take this leap of faith. But, after being obedient to his prompting, I knew I had made the right decision. I had taken off and soared like an eagle.

If you, like me, are struggling to step into God's calling for your life, then simply obey his voice and spread your wings! He will always be there to help you, and will never leave you to overcome the challenge on your own. When he calls us into the unknown, it can sometimes be really hard to trust him enough to take that leap of faith; it can be really scary to step out and spread one's wings. At times like this we need to remember that in all things, God sees the bigger picture. But if you obey his voice and do what he tells you to do, you will fly! Give it a go – it will be well worth it.

...but those who hope in the Lord will renew their strength. They will soar on wings like eagles; they will run and not grow weary, they will walk and not be faint. (Isaiah 40:31)

Testifying

When Jesus walked on the earth he proved through his miracles that he was the Son of God. He didn't do this once, but multiple times.

Sometimes it can be really difficult to explain to others who God is, as they simply can't or won't believe. It might feel like we will never get through to them. If we have a loved one, perhaps a friend or family member, who doesn't know God, then we need to tell them about him. And we need to make sure we don't give up if they don't understand straight away. Just like Jesus never lost patience or gave up on people, we too need to ask God to give us the perseverance to keep testifying about him.

Therefore go and make disciples of all nations, baptizing them in the name of the Father and of the Son and of the Holy Spirit..
(Matthew 28:19)

Never Too Young

God doesn't look at you and think, "I can't use her; she is too young." He sees you as his child, and can fully equip you to do the work he has called you to do. This doesn't depend on your age, your past, or even what you look like. Nothing else matters to him other than his relationship with you. He has called all of his children to tell others about him and thereby make disciples. No matter how challenging this calling may be, he will never ask us to do something that we can't handle.

I remember wondering about this very thing myself – had he given me something I couldn't do because of my youth and lack of experience? But God reminded me that he never calls us to do something that we aren't capable of doing; that he always gives us the ability to do what he asks of us. So if he tells you to pray for someone or to tell them about him, don't hold back because you think you can't do it. Don't let doubt or anxiety rob you of God's calling. He has a unique and specific plan for your life, and will equip you in every way to fulfil it. Just like Jesus, you are never too young to be about your Father's business.

Don't let anyone look down on you because you are young, but set an example for the believers in speech, in conduct, in love, in faith and in purity. (1 Timothy 4:12)

Repentance

Repentance is a wonderful thing. It entails admitting or confessing your sin (wrong doing and thinking) and turning back to doing what is good in God's sight. You now are forgiven and free!

When I was little I had such a strong repentant spirit. If I got into trouble at school or got up to mischief with my friends, I would always feel the need to admit it to my mum. I think that because I was young, I didn't understand that the Person I should be repenting to was God. Now that I'm older, I understand more fully just how important repentance is – it sets you free.

You can receive forgiveness from God simply by asking him for it. He will help you to not only forgive others but also forgive yourself. Nothing is too big or 'bad' to be forgiven. You may be wondering just how to repent. The following is what you could pray:

Dear God, I am sorry for the wrong I have thought or done. I am sorry for the good I have failed to do. Please forgive me and help me forgive myself. Thank you for your grace and love. Amen.

So, repent and ask God for forgiveness. He will set you free!

If we confess our sins, he is faithful and just and will forgive us our sins and purify us from all unrighteousness. (1 John 1:9)

Repent, then, *and turn to God, so that your sins may be wiped out, that times of refreshing may come from the Lord.* (Acts 3:19)

Jesus Wept

Sometimes life can be difficult to understand. You may wonder, "Why do bad things happen to good people? Why did God allow me to get hurt?" The answer to these questions is based on the incredible truth that he has given us *free will* to decide what we want to do in our lives. God loves us SO much that he won't force us to do anything, not even to love and obey him. By allowing us free will, he is allowing us to choose whether to sin or not. The consequences of sin are pain, loss, grief, sickness, violence and death.

God didn't choose our world to be like this – he created it to be a place where there was no sin or sorrow at all. When sin came into the world it greatly saddened him. He calls every one of us to turn away from sin and to repent, rather than face the dire consequences the evil of sin brings to our lives and the lives of those around us. When we go through challenges in life it is easy to get angry with God and sometimes even blame him for the bad things that happen. But we should know that he is perfect and there is no evil in him. He gives only what is good, and when we weep, he weeps with us.

His heart is soft and tender towards us, and our sorrows become his sorrows because of his great love for us. If we will only call out to him, then he will *deliver us from evil*. This is what Jesus taught us to pray in the Lord's Prayer.

When Jesus saw her weeping, and the Jews who had come along with her also weeping, he was deeply moved in spirit and troubled. "Where have you laid him?" he asked. "Come and see, Lord," they replied. Jesus wept.
(John 11:33-35)

In His Image

Self-image is something most people struggle with. I personally have always felt insecure about my skin and my weight. I've even at times been insecure about my intelligence. I have struggled with my own image and self-identity over the years. Almost everyone has at least one thing they feel insecure about. These usually stem from past experiences (whether they be conscious or unconscious memories), and it isn't your fault that you feel this way.

God doesn't intend us to be insecure. He created us in His image. He formed us in our mothers' wombs. His will is for us to be perfect, like he is. Thoughts of insecurity might creep into your head, but always remember – you are God's beautiful creation!

So God created mankind in his own image, in the image of God he created them; male and female he created them. (Genesis 1:27)

God's Goodness

I wonder if you have seen the movie *God's not Dead*? One of my favourite lines from it is, "God is good all the time, and all the time God is good." Yes, he is always good and will never fail us. God is perfect; there is no evil in him. And when our lives are difficult he can turn the problems into something good, if we bring them to him. It's never too late to turn to God. He is the one Person who will always be there for you and will never forsake you. When you ask him to forgive your sins, he will always be gracious and do just that. If you have rejected him or you just feel lost, I encourage you to turn to him – for he is eternally good. And he is longing to restore and heal you, and bring you into his presence, where there is fullness of joy. I hope you understand that it's never too late to receive his goodness. If you think you want to ask God into your life (either for the first time or once again, after wandering off), then please turn to the last page of this book, where you will find a simple prayer that you might like to use. Then, after you have made peace with him, it will be time to celebrate all the good things that he has in store for you!

Oh, give thanks to the Lord, for He is good! For His mercy endures forever. (1 Chronicles 16:34 NKJV)

Glory

God created you to be glorious! He wants you to reflect his glory. Jesus is our prime example in this. Wherever he walked, whoever he spoke to, and whatever he did, was done for the glory of God. We are called to be loving, kind, graceful and wise like him. If we become like him then unbelievers will see it and wonder how we are able to be like that. God tells us that we are to do everything for the glory of God – so that others will see God working through us. We are to be his ambassadors. This should influence the choices and decisions we make. One of the ways this can be done is by simply explaining who God is to a friend at school. Whatever you do, make sure you are a representation of God's glory. You have a job to do, so do it!

So whether you eat or drink or whatever you do, do it all for the glory of God. (1 Corinthians 10:31)

Before the Ring

Dating and relationships can not only be exciting, but may also teach us much. And once we have found the person God has matched us with, marriage will be beautiful.

Dating prepares us for marriage, right? Well, if so, what prepares us for dating? I believe that the best preparation for dating is based on two things – firstly, loving God, and secondly, loving ourselves. If you build a strong relationship with God before you start dating, then you will save yourself from making bad choices. God will give you the guidance you need in looking for your 'significant other'. He will give you wisdom when you're in doubt about the right choice to make. Once you have built a strong relationship with God, you will find that you automatically love yourself.

I have been in a few relationships in the past and, looking back, the thing I regret most is that I didn't have an adequate sense of self-worth at the time. This would have saved me a lot of pain. So, before *you* date someone, remember what is important – love for God and love for yourself.

For you created my inmost being; you knit me together in my mother's womb. I praise you because I am fearfully and wonderfully made; your works are wonderful, I know that full well. My frame was not hidden from you when I was made in the secret place, when I was woven together in the depths of the earth. (Psalm 139:13-15)

Above All Else

It is important to remember that the most important thing in your life is God. Choose him above all else. Above every earthly thing, whether it be small or big. It may be difficult to do this; it may involve going against the crowd. God wants you to follow him and not others.

I've had moments in life where I have followed the crowd, but in the end, it didn't sit right with God. He had called me to higher things. Just like me, he has called you to greater things. He has chosen you to be different, and to stand out in a crowd, to be a leader and not a follower. In times of temptation, choose him and he will give you strength to be a follower of him and not of the world.

Do not conform to the pattern of this world, but be transformed by the renewing of your mind. Then you will be able to test and approve what God's will is – his good, pleasing and perfect will. (Romans 12:2)

Shine!

God has called his children to be shining lights in this world; to be lamps in the darkness. This could be through the simple act of giving. My mum is a good example of shining her light in this way. She loves giving, whether it be through food, presents or, most importantly, her love. Through her giving she shines her light on Jesus. She doesn't take the credit, but explains that it's God's work.

Telling others about God is another way of shining our light. As Christians, we are all called to share the Good News so that others will know the goodness of God. So I encourage you to shine your light in the midst of the darkness in whatever way you can. You could try speaking some encouraging words to your friends, or helping in the community. Other people will see God working in you when you shine out his light!

In the same way, let your light shine before others, that they may see your good deeds and glorify your Father in heaven. (Matthew 5:16)

A Higher Plan

God has chosen a specific path for you! He has a plan of hope and purpose for your life. Every life has a different plan, and it may not be one you expect. It is common for young adults to plan their lives. They plan what year they will finish school, when they will go travelling, and even by what year they want to be married. Yes, some of our plans will eventuate, but most of them are fantasy.

It can be disappointing when at first our plans don't go the way we want. It may be that we don't get the job we want or if the relationship we think is *the* one fails. God's plan for our life is the best one for us, and each one is unique. If we want to live in obedience to him, then he will guide us into it. He wants to remind us that his plans are higher than our plans. That he has a greater plan for us, one that is better than we can imagine. Remember, you may make many plans for your life, but God's plan will ultimately prevail – if you trust him.

You can make many plans, but the LORD's purpose will prevail. (Proverbs 19:21 NLT)

declares the Lord, "plans to prosper you and not to harm you, plans to give you a hope and a future…" (Jeremiah 29:11)

The Waiting Room

I find it difficult to be patient in a waiting room. Patience is a gift that we need to ask God for. When we learn to wait in patience in life, beautiful things happen. An example of this is the time Mum and I set out to buy some feijoas. We drove down a country road where we knew people sold them. Five minutes down this road we came across the first bags of feijoas. The impatience in me made me decide that these were good enough, but in reality they were old and inedible. Mum knew to keep on driving. After another ten minutes of driving, we came to the second stop. Again I thought these were good enough, but again Mum felt that it would be better that we keep on driving. After another twenty minutes we came to the third stop, where there were beautiful, big feijoas. That day Mum taught me a lesson about patience.

I believe God calls us to be patient because he wants to test our faith. Patience saves us from difficult situations and leads us closer to God. Make sure that you grow in patience through waiting.

Be joyful in hope, patient in affliction, faithful in prayer. (Romans 12:12)

Wrong Direction

God has provided you a path that leads to your destination in him. But he has also given you the right to freedom of choice. You are free to make decisions that aren't in his calling for you and therefore won't take you in the right direction. But remember, God will always direct you back to your true destination, if you want him to! Think of it as a GPS system. When you're en route to a destination, the GPS will show you the most direct way to get there. If you decide to choose a different route, the GPS doesn't just stop working, but rather re-tracks and creates a new pathway to your chosen destination.

It is the same with God. If you take a different path to the one he has directed you on and have gone in the wrong direction, then don't worry. When you ask Him to, he will always re-direct you. He will provide a new route for you and thereby ensure you land up at your original destination. But it's your decision whether or not you want to go there.

I will instruct you and teach you in the way you should go; I will counsel you with my eye upon you. (Psalm 32:8 ESV)

Joy

Joy is deep inner pleasure. There is a difference in being happy and being joyful. Joy isn't based on circumstances, whereas happiness is. God offers us his Holy Spirit to live in us. He is full of love, joy and peace, and as he dwells in our hearts, they become joyful. Joy is a powerful thing to have, especially when we are going through challenging times.

How can you receive this joy? Firstly, you have to acknowledge that deep inner joy comes from him. Nothing and no one else can bring you pure joy. Yes, other things can make you happy; but God is the one that transforms your happiness into joy. It's tricky to work out what makes you the happiest. You might think your friends make you the happiest - or your family, your dog or your school. Or maybe even your 'significant other'. But when you understand that joy comes from God alone then it becomes an everlasting treasure to be desired. Every earthly thing is temporary, but God is forever. Remember, when life gets hard, ask God for inner joy!

May the God of hope fill you with all joy and peace as you trust in him, so that you may overflow with hope by the power of the Holy Spirit. (Romans 15:13)

After the Battle

Trials and battles in life have a purpose. But while we are going through a dark season, we usually can't see the light at the end of the tunnel. But God uses our trials and battles and turns them into good. They can serve to make us stronger people, and afterwards they become battle scars that serve to help other people who have suffered in a similar way and who desperately need to hear how we survived our battle. Your tough times will be used to help them through their tough times.

There is a story in the Bible about a man called Lazarus. Lazarus was sick and eventually died, but Jesus raised him from the dead. God was able to use Lazarus' suffering to perform a miracle. Many people saw God's goodness and glorified him for the healing. Many people believed that Jesus was the Messiah because of this miracle. Similarly in our own lives, when we go through a difficult time, we can ask God to create goodness out of it. Don't lose hope when you are in those hard times, but know that after the battle is over and has been won, you will be able to help others. They will be able to see God's goodness in bringing you through victoriously.

Consider it pure joy, my brothers and sisters, whenever you face trials of many kinds, because you know that the testing of your faith produces perseverance. (James 1:2-3)

Mountain-Climbing

In Philippians 4:13, Paul talks about how we can do all things through Christ as he gives us strength. This scripture tells us about how God can help us through anything, especially through overcoming our biggest fears. When I think about it I get a picture of someone climbing a mountain. I personally have a fear of heights, and whenever I went rock-climbing this scripture would come to mind. It's different for everyone. My brother would think about it when he sat exams.

Some things seem impossible, and we question how we can achieve them by ourselves. We may get help from others, but the greatest strength we can grab onto is God's. When you are fearful, pray and ask him to give you strength. God is right next to us in every step we take. With him all things are possible as he gives us strength to do them.

I can do all this through him, who gives me strength. (Philippians 4:13)

Just Ask Jesus

Prayer is a key part of having a relationship with Jesus Christ. Sometimes we can overthink praying. How *do* we pray? What do we say? How long does it have to be? Questions like these may be confusing and put us off praying altogether. But know this - prayer is much more simple than you realise. God wants a *relationship* with you, just like you would have with a best friend. All you need to do is talk to him, however you want to. There are no rules. Speak to him about anything and everything, in any way you want to.

If you regularly pray to God, you will get to know him better. Talk to him about your day. He will reveal things to you about himself and about yourself that you didn't know before. He will answer your prayers in ways you can't even imagine. And praying for others will change their lives too. Everyone has a need in their life, and your prayers will help them get the answer they need. So pray. Get to know Jesus, and go to him in prayer for yourself and for others.

Then you will call on me and come and pray to me, and I will listen to you. (Jeremiah 29:12)

Representing God's Love

Jesus taught us that the greatest commandment of all was to love God, and that the next greatest was to love your neighbour (representing everyone you come across in your daily life) as much as you love yourself. You may have heard about this in Sunday School or from reading the Bible. But if you have never heard this before, that's okay!

Why should we treat people the way *we* want to be treated, even when we don't know them? It may seem crazy to be expected to be kind to strangers, but God has called us to be different - to be a light in the darkness and thereby to represent him. God is full of pure love and selflessness. He sent his Son Jesus to die for us. Just as he loves us, so we are called to love others.

We don't know other people's circumstances, and we may never know how our kindness and love have impacted their lives. God wants to use us to help other people, and that can be done by treating everyone we come across with kindness, respect and love. If you know someone is in a difficult situation, try thinking about how best you could help them. In this way you will be representing God's love to them, and they will get to see him in you.

A new command I give you: Love one another. As I have loved you so you must love one another. (John 13:34)

Save Our Souls

Have you ever felt you were in a situation where you needed God to save you - an SOS (Save Our Souls) moment? When we pray and ask God to answer our prayers, we might have high expectations of how he is going to answer. We might expect it to be something out of the ordinary, when in reality he might answer by sending us something unexceptional or someone we didn't expect.

Have you heard the story of the girl who was stranded on an island? This young woman had faith that God had heard her prayer, and was waiting for an extraordinary way of being saved. So when a man came past in his boat and offered to rescue her, she declined, explaining that she was waiting for God to save her. Then a cruise ship came past, and after that a plane. She declined both of these too, as she believed God would save her in an extraordinary way. She then asked God why he hadn't yet saved her, and he told her he had sent out three rescue attempts already. What else did she want?

Of course this is an allegory, and not a true account, but it does illustrate the point. When we ask God to save us from situations, we need to be open to whatever and whoever he sends to help us. Our prayer might well be answered differently to what we expect, and we don't want to miss God's answer.

And whatever you ask in my name, that will I do, that the Father may be glorified in the Son. (John 14:13 NKJV)

Whoops!

Mistakes happen all the time. They don't happen purposefully; we don't intend them to take place. Everyone makes mistakes, and it's important to know that it's normal to have 'whoopsie' moments now and then, or to make life choices that are later proved to be bad ones. We can easily be discouraged, and blame ourselves for mistakes we have made in the past. And that's when God wants to remind us of who he is and how much he loves us. Yes, we aren't perfect, but God loves us all the same. He loves us enough to take care of our flaws or our everyday mistakes, and to set us free from them.

Draw near to God when you realise you have made a mistake. If you feel you want to go to someone, then talk to a friend or spiritual leader about it. Ask God to direct you to someone who can guide you through steps of repentance and in knowing his forgiveness. Mistakes happen all the time, so don't beat yourself up. Remember, God sees you as his wonderful daughter.

If we confess our sins, he is faithful and just and will forgive us our sins and purify us from all unrighteousness. (1 John 1:9)

Begin Again

Sometimes our faith may be weak. Like a fire, it can burn low. This often happens when life gets busy, and we find it difficult to manage the load of school, work, and a social life without leaving God out of it. I remember coming home from a church camp and feeling 'on fire' for God. This feeling lasted for a while, but gradually weakened as my life became busier. I had forgotten to set aside time each day for spending with God.

So what should we do when we have lost our hunger for God? How do we get it back? Just like a car needs to fill up on fuel every so often, so we too need to refuel our flame for God. By setting aside time every day to spend with him we can do just that. Maybe you could spend time with him every morning just after you wake up, or every night before you go to sleep. Spend some time praying and reading his Word each day. I know this can be hard to fit in when one has a busy schedule, but it is worth it.

A tip to succeed at this is to set yourself reminders. Maybe place your Bible next to your bed so that you will remember to read it. Don't worry if you have lost your flame for God - you can always begin again.

Therefore we do not lose heart. Though outwardly we are wasting away, yet inwardly we are being renewed day by day. For our light and momentary troubles are achieving for us an eternal glory that far outweighs them all. (2 Corinthians 4:16-17)

The Ways of the World

When going through our teenage years in high school, we will be exposed to the ways of the world. These ways are stereotypically 'normal' to a non-Christian. They often include activities such as drinking alcohol, smoking and engaging in sexual encounters. Christians, however, are called to follow a different path - one of righteousness, purity and faith.

I remember going to a party in my last year of high school. To others it seemed normal, but to me it wasn't. Smoking and getting drunk was normal fun to them, and it made them happy. However, they didn't have inner joy. We can only receive true joy from God. He alone fills up our love tanks. Non-Christians searching for an answer turn to the ways of the world as they know no other way. We are blessed to know the Truth, Jesus Christ himself. We need to encourage others to turn to him too.

So flee youthful passions and pursue righteousness, faith, love, and peace, along with those who call on the Lord from a pure heart. (2 Timothy 2:22 ESV)

Graciousness

There is a particular story in the Bible that depicts just how gracious Jesus is. A woman was brought before Jesus as a means of trapping him into saying something the Pharisees could hold against him. She had committed adultery, and they wanted to stone her to death as a punishment. When they asked Jesus what he thought they should do, he responded by saying, "Let the one who has never sinned throw the first stone!" One by one they left the scene, as each one realised they were sinful too.

Jesus was teaching us that before we judge others, we need to acknowledge that we too are all sinners. He had mercy on the woman and told her he didn't condemn her either. And, just as importantly, he also told her to stop sinning. We aren't perfect either. Sinning is a part and parcel of being human. We try not to sin, but when we do, we know God is gracious and will forgive us, when we ask him to.

They kept demanding an answer, so he stood up again and said, "All right, but let the one who has never sinned throw the first stone!" (John 8:7 NLT)

For Such a Time

Isn't God's timing amazing? It is easy to struggle over figuring out when something is going to happen. I know, as I have been there myself.

In the Old Testament we read the story of Esther, a Jewess who was married to the Persian king. Under the influence of an evil man, he ordered the annihilation of Jews throughout the empire. At great risk to her life, Esther felt convicted by God to persuade him to retract this order. Esther's cousin Mordecai convinced her to fulfil her calling, saying, "For if you remain silent at this time, relief and deliverance for the Jews will arise from another place, but you and your father's family will perish. And who knows but that you have come to your royal position for such a time as this?" Esther listened to Mordecai and persuaded the king to set the Jews free. God's timing was perfect, and Esther was used to free God's children.

We often don't understand God's timing, nor why we may be in a difficult season in our life. But we need to remember that if we have surrendered our lives to him, then this dark and perplexing time is fully in his hands. He will see us through to victory. God's timing is always perfect, and we can trust him to work things out perfectly for us.

> *"For if you remain silent at this time, relief and deliverance for the Jews will arise from another place, but you and your father's family will perish. And who knows but that you have come to your royal position for such a time as this?"* (Esther 4:14)

Called

God has a calling (a plan and a purpose) for every one of his children. This calling may entail us first having to give up a certain thing, or overcoming our biggest fear. God doesn't want fear to stop us from fulfilling that calling. So sometimes we will have to first face our fears in order to fulfil our calling. This can be scary - but God has a plan for that too. If you are confused about your calling, then wait. Pray, and he will answer. He will show you what he has called you to do and how to set about doing it.

I believe all of us are called to three important things in our lives, over and above our individual personal callings. The first two are Jesus' commandments to us - to love God and to love others, and the third is the Great Commission of Jesus - to spread the Good News of his kingdom throughout all the world.

When Jesus was asked what the greatest commandment in the law was, he replied, "Love the Lord your God with all your heart and with all your soul and with all your mind." The second calling refers to the second greatest commandment of Jesus, which is to love your neighbour as yourself. These two commandments are our first two callings. Our last calling was given by Jesus when he appeared to his disciples after having risen from the dead. He told them to go out into all the world and tell others the good news of his kingdom.

These are the three fundamental callings I adhere to in my life, and the foundation of being a follower of Jesus Christ. Now you too go and live out your calling!

"Therefore go and make disciples of all nations, baptizing them in the name of the Father and of the Son and of the Holy Spirit, and teaching them to obey everything I have commanded you. And surely I am with you always, to the very end of the age." (Matthew 28:19-20)

Real Love

Have you ever wanted to experience real love? The kind of love that is so powerful it can overcome anything. The kind of love that fills your heart and makes you secure. This is the kind of love we can only receive from God. We may search for love from others but, despite the best we may receive, it will never fully satisfy. I too have tried fulfilling my heart with the acceptance and love of others, but I have learnt there is no love like the love of God. He loved us before we were born, and will love us for the rest of our lives. He loves us so much that he sent his Son Jesus to die for us.

Jesus gave us a parable to explain just how much God loves each and every one of us. There was a shepherd (representing God) who had 100 sheep. One of them went missing. So he left the 99 other sheep to look for this lost one (representing each one of us). Remember, if you feel far from God, he loves you so much that he leaves everything else in order to find you. Even though we fail him every day, his grace overrides all of our sin. His love is pure and real. Ask him to show you his love. He loves you so much that he will do just that.

Anyone who does not love does not know God, because God is love. In this the love of God was made manifest among us, that God sent his only Son into the world, so that we might live through him. In this is love, not that we have loved God but that he loved us and sent his Son to be the propitiation for our sins. Beloved, if God so loved us, we also ought to love one another. (John 4:8-11 ESV)

Be Bold!

Boldness changes lives. One second of boldness in one person's life could result in an answered prayer in someone else's. Speaking to another person about God can be terrifying, especially when you think they don't want to hear it. Most people feel this way when they start spreading the Good News. But God has called us to be bold, to step out and be different. He equips us to be an example and a light to people who are lost. He calls us to be bold in telling others about him. How about telling someone about your own personal faith, or asking them if they would like you to pray for them? Being bold could look like being a part of the worship team or becoming a leader within the church. It could even look like complimenting a stranger or introducing yourself to the new kid at school. You never know what God will do through this simple act of boldness. I encourage you to be bold and see what happens. You could change someone's life!

In the day when I cried out, You answered me, And made me bold with strength in my soul. (Psalm 138:3 NKJV)

Princess and the Frog

The Princess and the Frog is a well-known children's story. When I was 16 years old my English teacher asked a question that explained it in a different way. Why kiss a frog before kissing the prince? It suddenly dawned on me that a princess should keep herself pure for her future husband.

God tells us in the Bible that we need to keep our bodies pure and holy as they are temples of the Holy Spirit. God has intended us to stay pure until we are married. So why throw away our kisses? We are daughters in Christ. We wear his royal crown on our heads. We ought not to be throwing away our purity. Physical intimacy belongs to a relationship with our future husband. So keep your kisses close. Don't throw them away on a frog, but rather save them for your prince.

Do you not know that your bodies are temples of the Holy Spirit, who is in you, whom you have received from God? You are not your own; you were bought at a price. Therefore honour God with your bodies. (1 Corinthians 6:19-20)

Royal Crown

If you could only see yourself the way God sees you! You are his royal princess. You are always wearing his crown on your head. You can't do anything to make him LOVE you more because he already loves you so much. In him we find our identity. We are his royal daughters in Christ.

God wants us to find our self-worth in him. Don't go searching for your identity in any other person than God. No activity, desire or person will fulfil your self-esteem like God will. Ask him to show you the way he sees you. The almighty God has a specific plan for your life. He loves you that much. Don't allow anyone to make you feel like you are not worthy. The best thing about God's love is that we don't have to earn it. And we don't have to earn our identity. We were given it the moment we were born again. Remember that as a Christian you wear God's crown on your head, and your identity is found in Christ.

For you created my inmost being; you knit me together in my mother's womb. (Psalm 139:13)

Relational Faith

My family has been taking me to church ever since I was born. But it wasn't until I was around 14 years old that I gained a valuable perspective. Being part of a church community creates relational faith – a faith journey that is no longer just you and God, but linked with other like-minded people on the same journey. God calls us to have relational faith and to grow together in Christ.

I encourage you to start participating in your local church. Make connections with other like-minded people, and consider serving where you feel you can contribute according to your gifting. Praying and seeking God together with others will help to build your personal relationship with God. In this way you will feel supported and encouraged to continue growing in your faith. Remember, whilst it's great to attend church, it's even better to serve within that church – not only does it benefit others, but it also helps you connect to those around you and to start having relational faith. Now go and connect with your fellow believers!

For where two or three gather in my name, there am I with them." (Matthew 18:20)

Chickens

Over the last couple of months I have been working part-time in a clothing store to save up for university. Me being my organised self, I would calculate how much money I would be paid before I had even worked the week. Soon I realised that by doing so I was counting my chickens before they had hatched! This valuable an old saying tells us *not* to 'count our chickens before they hatch' and, as my mum explained, that means not projecting an outcome based on what you think you are seeing before the event takes place - given that you will probably be disappointed with a very different outcome.

God is the master-planner, and his purposes will always prevail. We should not build unrealistic expectations in things in our life such as friendships, income, relationships and school. And besides, even if our expectations aren't met, there is no need to worry because God has our backs! We have to learn to trust in him and not in our own understanding of things! In moments of disappointment, give your expectations to God and allow him to guide you on your path.

Trust in the LORD with all your heart and lean not on your own understanding; in all your ways submit to him, and he will make your paths straight. (Proverbs 3:5-6)

Open Doors

When I was growing up, my mum always told me that when one door closes another one opens in its place. She would relate this to situations such as not getting a job I was hoping for, the ending of a friendship I had treasured, and having a boy stop liking me.

At the end of the day you should know that God has set specific doors for you to go through that will lead to his purposes being fulfilled in your life. There will be open doors, closed doors and those doors that you have the option to open or close. If you feel like something hasn't gone to plan, or you didn't get an opportunity you wanted, consider it a door closed. If you look to God, you will find that in time a new one opens in its place. You may need to try new things to discover what God has planned for you. But don't worry! God will open the right doors for you.

"I know all the things you do, and I have opened a door for you that no one can close. You have little strength, yet you obeyed my word and did not deny me." (Revelation 3:8 NLT)

Pointless Worry

In Matthew chapter six Jesus talks about the pointlessness of worrying. He explains that we do not have to worry about what we eat, what we drink or what we wear. Jesus is explaining that we do not have to worry about the basic necessities of life as he will provide us with everything we need.

I have recently been worrying about my university work, mainly around getting assignments done. Worrying to the point of nearly having a mental breakdown. I realise I should be over worrying about these things because God tells us clearly that we should *not* worry about this kind of stuff.

You too don't need to worry about what is happening at school or over which outfit you should choose to wear. Nor do you need to worry about the future. About what's happening tomorrow, next week or even next month. It's easy to worry about situations that haven't even happened yet! God doesn't want us to worry about the future as he wants us to enjoy the present. If you are sick and tired of worrying about both the big and small things in life, then take heart! Give those worries to God, and ask him to take full control of all of your life.

Therefore do not worry about tomorrow, for tomorrow will worry about itself. Each day has enough trouble of its own.
(Matthew 6:34)

Modest is Hottest

'Modest is hottest' is a saying I heard in church whilst growing up. It suggests that girls who dress modestly are considered to be more attractive than those who 'show more skin.'

By the time they get to high school, most girls have started dressing provocatively, notably at parties and at popular hang-outs, and at school on mufti days. When I was growing up I was upset that my non-Christian friends were able to wear crop-tops, whereas I was told I couldn't. I was only trying to fit in and be considered pretty. But God explains that true beauty is found on the inside and not in our outward appearance. He looks at our hearts. We should be looking for God's approval, not anyone else's. We need to be worried about the condition of our hearts rather than picking a cute outfit to impress others.

Charm is deceitful, and beauty is fleeting, but a woman who fears the Lord is to be praised.
(Proverbs 31:30)

Stand Up

Bullies are mean and nasty; they put you down and make you feel worthless. Bullying takes many forms, including leaving someone out, 'joking' by calling them names, or spreading rumours about them. I got bullied in Year 10 at school. I was often left out of things and had people talking behind my back, and as a result felt worthless all the time.

God doesn't want us to be bullied, nor does he want us to feel worthless. He has called us to be his children, and to stand up for ourselves and others. One way of de-escalating a bad situation is to leave the scene and thereby stay out of the drama. Or we could be honest and express how we feel. We could 'kill them with kindness'. God says that instead of being angry, we should be kind to one another and forgive each other. It may be hard, but we do have to forgive the bully. Ask God to help you do this. Stand up for yourself and forgive him or her, just as Christ has forgiven you.

Get rid of all bitterness, rage and anger, brawling and slander, along with every form of malice. Be kind and compassionate to one another, forgiving each other, just as in Christ God forgave you.(Ephesians 4:31-32)

Lies

Did you know that when you think negative thoughts, that is often the devil putting lies in your head. He is real, and he tries to take over your mind. He likes to make you feel insecure.

One of the lies I have been believing is that I am unintelligent. This makes me feel that I'm not good enough or smart enough for anyone else. Recently, however, I have been realising that these feelings are the devil's lies, and that they are not the truth.

Everyone has strengths and weaknesses. The devil knows our strengths, and tries to tell us that our strengths are actually weaknesses. This can leave us feeling defeated. God, on the other hand, will always tell us the truth. He reminds us what is true about ourselves and assures us that we need never be insecure about anything. In John 14:6, Jesus tells us that he is the Way, the Truth and the Life. All we need to do is rely on his truth in and about every situation in our lives.

If you feel like the devil is whispering lies in your head, ask God what the truth is - I can guarantee it will be the opposite of what the devil has been telling you. Then you will be able to find strength in God and stand up to his lies.

Finally, be strong in the Lord and in his mighty power. Put on the full armor of God, so that you can take your stand against the devil's schemes. (Ephesians 6:10-11 NIV)

But the Lord is faithful, and he will strengthen you and protect you from the evil one. (2 Thessalonians 3:3)

Contentment

I often struggled to feel content whilst growing up. I always felt like I needed to be doing something; when I wasn't, I would freak out! I wasn't content with just living my day as it came. Contentment is signified by feelings of satisfaction and happiness.

God calls us to be content, and not to worry, stress or over-plan our lives. If I am content in my relationship with him, then he will give me contentment in my life. He will provide us with contentment if we ask him to.

Sometimes I have to remind myself that God created all living things and every single day. He doesn't want us to worry about earthly things because when we get to heaven, none of it will matter anymore. As long as we have the necessities of life, we don't need to worry about anything else. If you feel like you are discontented, ask God to help you! He will provide everything you need in life so that you can be content.

But godliness with contentment is great gain. For we brought nothing into the world, and we can take nothing out of it. But if we have food and clothing, we will be content with that. (1 Timothy 6:6-8)

Children of God

One of the greatest things God offers us is a secure personal identity. I personally have struggled with knowing who I am and what my label is.

God has created each one of us, and we were born for a purpose. That purpose includes being a light in the darkness and bringing other people to him. And many other wonderful and uniquely personal purposes too. God purposed us to be born in his perfect timing. And he doesn't want us to settle for anything less than his very best. We need to find our self-worth in him. I like to think that God places crowns on our heads and calls us his princesses. Whenever I struggle with feelings of not being good enough, I think about that crown on my head and remember I am worthy because I am a child of the king! We are his priceless gems. Our identity determines how we live our lives. Seek God, and find your identity in him. You are his child!

So in Christ Jesus you are all children of God through faith... (Galatians 3:26)

Acceptance

Everyone needs to feel the acceptance of other people in their lives. Without this, one can feel hopeless or worthless. But it is important to understand just *where* and *where not* to find that acceptance.

It's tempting to try to find acceptance through other people's opinions of us, and social media can easily become the place we go to find this acceptance. I am guilty of trying to find fulfilment through social media, and in caring about how many 'likes' I receive. However, God is the only one in whom we will find true acceptance. He made us from the dust of the ground, and has moulded us (and continues to mould us) to be who he wants us to be. He always accepts us, despite knowing our faults. And Jesus is the perfect example of how to accept others. Just as he has accepted us, so we are called to accept others.

If you are struggling to feel accepted by God or by other people, ask him to show you just how much he loves you! Then, just as God accepts you, accept others too!

Accept one another, then, just as Christ accepted you, in order to bring praise to God. (Romans 15:7)

Powerful Words

Do you know the power of the spoken word? There is incredible weight in our words, so it is important that we speak life and truth over ourselves and others! When I was in high school my mum reminded me every morning to have courage and to be kind, and those words influenced my behaviour greatly.

When speaking words over yourself, you must remember the importance of speaking God's truth. If we are speaking things over our lives that don't line up with God's truth, then we will end up believing lies about ourselves. If we tell ourselves 'I *can* do it' then we will be able to do it. And, conversely, if we tell ourselves the opposite then we will be discouraged.

So I encourage you to speak only positive words over yourself and your friends. Every morning when you wake up or when you are on your way to school, tell yourself 'I can do it.' 'I am beautiful and worthy' and, most importantly, 'I am a child of God'. Speak God's truth over yourself!

Gracious words are a honeycomb, sweet to the soul and healing to the bones. (Proverbs 16:24)

Gentle words are a tree of life; a deceitful tongue crushes the spirit. (Proverbs 15:4 NLT)

Rest

Whilst growing up I constantly struggled to sit down and rest. I was always worrying about the next thing I had to do and where I needed to go. This anxiety increased during high school, and persisted to my time at university. To be honest, I still struggle with it even today, and it's still a daily battle for me to take time to rest.

God encourages us to take time to rest in our busy lives. He knows just how important it is. He even created a whole day each week for rest. A Sabbath day for us to praise him and find rest in him.

Time in his presence reminds us that we need to take life slowly and not to sweat the small stuff. Even when our lives are busy, Jesus has open arms for us to come to and find rest in. You don't have to be at church to be filled up with his restful presence. All you need to do is put some worship music on, start praying about your day and start to relax. You will find rest for your body, soul and spirit in him.

"Come to me, all you who are weary and burdened, and I will give you rest. Take my yoke upon you and learn from me, for I am gentle and humble in heart, and you will find rest for your souls. For my yoke is easy and my burden is light." (Matthew 11:28-30)

Blessed is She

We are so blessed! Do you know why you are blessed? Because you have the King of all kings, Jesus Christ, as your Saviour! As Christians, we are blessed to know God's promises for our lives. We know he has a wonderful plan for us, and that because of this we can give him full control of our lives. He brings us security, and a hope for the future. How difficult life must be for those people who don't know God and how much he loves them. We are fortunate because we know that God has control over our lives! We are blessed because we don't have to worry about the little things, or about our future. Consider yourself blessed that you have security in God's promises. If you have a friend who doesn't have the blessing of knowing God, then tell them about his love! We are blessed to be a blessing to others. Ask God to help you tell others about him so that they can believe his promises too. And rejoice in that you are blessed!

...Blessed is she who has believed that the Lord would fulfil his promises to her" (Luke 1:45)

Overcoming Fear

Something that has been on my heart recently is our need to give our fears to God. Everyone deals with fears. You might have a fear of heights or of spiders. And then there are the bigger and deeper fears we all face, such as fear of failure, loneliness and rejection. It's easy to become fearful, and most of us even consider it 'normal.' However, that is not how God created us to be. He created us to be strong and fearless. It's easy to fall into a slump of fear when you are uncertain about your future. If you're at school and you are fearful about the future, don't worry! God is in control of all situations.

A good way to overcome fear is to praise. We have the power to praise God instead of being fearful. This can be done by turning on worship music in your room, or listening to it on your way to school. This allows the Holy Spirit to calm you. It reminds you that fear isn't what God intends for you.

God created us to be fearless!

When you next are feeling a sense of fear, pray and give it to God. Next, turn some worship music on and sing praises to him. God will take away your fears if you ask him to!

Finally, brothers and sisters, whatever is true, whatever is noble, whatever is right, whatever is pure, whatever is lovely, whatever is admirable - if anything is excellent or praiseworthy - think about such things. (Philippians 4:8)

Consistency

Life can be messy. An organised person like myself needs things to be in order. Unfortunately life isn't perfect, and it often gets out of control - and that's not our fault. If there is drama at school or at home, it can feel like life will always stay messy. That's not the truth!

In moments of craziness it can become confusing knowing who to turn to for consistency and order. God is always consistent and is the same every day. He has called you to live in his consistency. He will forever be a rock to lean on in times of craziness and disorder. He will always be gracious, forgiving and good. If you feel like you are drowning in the messiness of life, pray to Jesus. He has your back in every situation. You can rely on him to be your rock as he is the same yesterday, today and forever.

Jesus Christ is the same yesterday and today and forever. (Hebrews 13:8)

Gratitude

One day when I was taking my dog for a walk through the bush, I noticed how many times he stopped to smell things. It dawned on me that animals take time to stop and smell the plants, trees and sometimes even the flowers.

In our journey in life we too need to stop sometimes and just smell the flowers. To stop, take a deep breath, and remember how grateful we should be. It's easy to think about all the things we don't have, and to forget how much we do have. God has blessed us with so much! He has blessed us with friends and family! With food and water! He has blessed us with a beautiful planet! Instead of asking God for more, just stop and remember how much he has already given you. I encourage you to write a list of at least five things you are thankful for. Just stop for a moment and be grateful.

Now then, stand still and see this great thing the LORD is about to do before your eyes! (1 Samuel 12:16)

Give Your Heart

Giving your heart to the Lord is the best decision you could ever make! Once you ask Jesus to be a part of your life, you will be blessed with everything he has in store for you. You will find your purpose and calling. You will find confidence and security. You will be able to live out your identity as a child of God! He is your best friend and he will walk alongside you every single day. He is with you 24/7, and is always there to talk to. Giving your heart to the Lord will result in your having a forever best friend to do life with! If you want to be best friends with God, simply pray this prayer:

Dear Jesus, I come to you as I need you in my life. I believe that you are the Son of God and the King of all kings. Come into my life. I give my heart to you. Forgive me my sins as I have sinned against you. Fill me with your love, and help me to live in obedience to you. May I live out the calling you created just for me. I love you with my heart, soul and mind. I thank you that now I am your child, and a princess of almighty King Jesus. Amen.

For God so loved the world that he gave his one and only Son, that whoever believes in him shall not perish but have eternal life. (John 3:16)

www.ingramcontent.com/pod-product-compliance
Lightning Source LLC
Chambersburg PA
CBHW062052290426
44109CB00027B/2805